Cicadas don't bug me

Written by **CHRISTEN JESCHKE**

FREILING PUBLISHING

Published by Freiling Publishing, a division of Freiling Agency, LLC.

P.O. Box 1264, Warrenton, VA 20188

www.FreilingPublishing.com

ISBN 978-1-950948-74-1

Printed in the United States of America
Designed by Debbie Lewis

To my sister, Katherine Craddock,
whose feelings for cicadas
inspired me to write this book.

What are the insects circling the skies?

They are very big with large glowing eyes.

DID YOU KNOW: Cicadas have no natural predators. Due to their abundance and clumsy flying, cicadas are an easy snack for birds, reptiles, fish, mammals, and other insects.

A cicada....
that seems an
odd-sounding word.

Is it true they
are food for the
hungriest bird?

DID YOU KNOW: Cicadas begin as an egg before hatching into a nymph. They live as nymphs underground for years. Cicadas moult their exoskeletons on plants or trees, emerging as adults.

First an egg,
then a nymph
underground.

Molting their
skin, they make
their first sound.

The song of the cicada
is loud like a screech.

The male screams
to a mate out of
his reach.

The female answers back
with a trill of her wings,

All through the day, the
mating call sings.

DID YOU KNOW: Cicadas are loud. The male cicada uses organs on their abdomen called tymbals to produce a variety of calls, including the mating call. Female cicadas respond to this call by making a flicking sound with their wings.

Cicadas are thirsty,
drinking until

The sap of the trees
gives them their fill.

DID YOU KNOW: Cicadas have a straw
shaped mouth which prevents them
from chewing. Instead, they pierce
plants and trees with their stylet to
drink watery sap called xylem.

Their mouth is shaped like the tube of a straw.

Slurping their food, they can't bite you at all.

Cicadas may look ugly
or scary at first,

They won't hurt you, so
they're far from the worst.

DID YOU KNOW: The average cicada
is less than two inches long.

So don't bug out if a cicada is near,

You're bigger and stronger, there's no need to fear.

DID YOU KNOW: Cicadas have five eyes. They have two large compound eyes and three tiny eyes called ocelli.

There may be a large swarm
but soon you will see.

They are only here for a
visit, so just let them be.

DID YOU KNOW: Periodical cicadas emerge every thirteen or seventeen years as a large swarm called a brood. The lifespan of an adult periodical cicada is four to six weeks. Annual and Protoperiodical cicadas emerge yearly.

Wonder and marvel
as they fly around,

Soon they'll be gone and
you won't hear a sound.

The whispers of
cicadas are left
in the trees,

Exoskeletons
cling as they waft
in the breeze.

DID YOU KNOW: Cicadas may look intimidating, but they don't bite or sting and are not harmful to humans. In fact, some humans actually eat them, incorporating them into a variety of meals. Cicada ice cream anyone?

Gather your buckets and
collect what you find.

Discover with friends
cicada shells left behind.

Cicadas don't bug me.
They are fascinating teachers.

There's so much to learn
from these
curious creatures.

CPSIA information can be obtained
at www.ICGtesting.com
Printed in the USA
BVHW021914030521
606358BV00002B/6